A SWING FOR
A LIFETIME

GOLF DIGEST LEARNING LIBRARY
VOLUME 1

A SWING FOR A LIFETIME

*How you can build one and make it
repeat with this proven method from
the game's greatest teachers*

BOB TOSKI and JIM FLICK
with Larry Dennis
illustrations by Elmer Wexler

POCKET BOOKS
New York   London   Toronto   Sydney   Tokyo   Singapore

Published by:

Golf Digest/Tennis, Inc.
A New York Times Company,
5520 Park Avenue, Box 395
Trumbull, CT 06611-0395

and

POCKET BOOKS, a division of Simon & Schuster Inc.
1230 Avenue of the Americas
New York, NY 10020

Illustrations by Elmer Wexler

Book Design by Laura Hough

Cover Photograph by Dom Furore

ISBN: 0-671-75869-1

First Golf Digest/Tennis, Inc. and Pocket Books
trade paperback printing April 1992

10 9 8 7 6 5 4 3 2 1

Printed in the U.S.A.

CONTENTS

1

GOLF IS A TARGET GAME, TOO

Sam Snead once said at a meeting of the Golf Digest Professional Panel that during his lifetime he had played almost every sport, and he found golf to be the most difficult. That's not hard to understand when you consider the various complexities of the game—the different swings, the different playing fields, the varying conditions. It becomes even easier to understand when you realize the problem golfers face—they are essentially going about their business blindly.

In almost every game there is a target. In most of them, the player reacts to his target while he's looking at it. That's true in trapshooting, baseball, football, basketball, bowling, billiards, tennis and about every other target-oriented sport you can imagine.

It's not true in golf. Golf is certainly a target game, too. But the golfer is not looking at the target while he's in action. The things the golfer must do to prepare his or her body to get the ball to the target are done while looking at the

ball. That's a big difference.

The physical action in most games is one of reaction. The baseball pitcher sees the plate and reacts by throwing the ball over it. The hitter sees the ball coming in and reacts by swinging. The football quarterback sees his receiver and reacts by throwing to him. The receiver sees the ball coming and reacts by catching it...if it isn't batted down first by the defensive back who also is reacting to the ball. The basketball player reacts to the hoop by throwing the ball through it. The tennis player, always in motion, reacts to the ball coming at him, which is his first target, and hits it across the net to the spot he's aiming for in the opponent's court. That's his second target.

In almost all cases, the athlete is in motion before and while he makes the action that accomplishes his purpose. Even marksmen—trapshooters, riflemen, pistol shooter, archers—while they are still prior to the act, are able to see and focus their minds on their targets, letting their nerves and muscles react to that mental picture.

The golfer, on the other hand, has a twofold problem. He is basically motionless prior to the swing, and at the moment of the swing he does not have a target to react to. Some wise man once declared that golf is a game of *creation* rather than *reaction*. In essence, that's true. You must react to the target if you are to make a successful shot, but because you go from a standing start and because you are not watching the target, you must, in essence, create that reaction.

The unsuccessful player cannot do that. We see too many amateurs who stand fixed at address, and that static position soon becomes rigidity. Tension soon floods their muscles. They rivet their eyes on the ball, and you just know that the target is the farthest thing from their minds. Their sole focus is on the ball and, undoubtedly, on the swing mechanics they'll have to make to strike that ball. They have become "ball-bound," and when they finally do get the swing started it usually is with a rigid lurch that results in an awkward swipe at the ball with no idea where it is going or where they want it to. Consequently, it almost always goes where they don't want it to...if it goes very far at all.

The successful player, on the other hand, is able to create the proper reaction by a series of mental and physical maneuvers that keep his mind attuned to the target and his muscles free of tension so he can create a fluid and effective swing. He doesn't swing at the ball. He swings *through* it, sending it on its way to the target he has picked out. That's why every phase of the Golf Digest Schools concept and program has been established to simulate the way good players play the game. Simply stated, that's feeling the swing and reacting to the target.

How to React to the Target

You react to different targets in different ways—with different concepts and different strokes.

For example, the target on the green is not much bigger than a mason jar. So you have to set that target firmly in your mind's eye. Determine the direction and sense how far you have to make the ball go. With the putter, you want to make contact at the bottom of your swing arc. Getting the ball to

4

roll the correct distance will be determined by solid contact and the speed and length of your stroke. Again, that speed and length is ingrained by practice, but it's always a result of your reaction to the target.

On your shot to the green, you have a larger target, the green itself. Again, you have to define that target and set it in your mind. You want the ball to fly in a predetermined manner by controlling the club through proper use of the hands and arms. In this case, especially with a short iron, you want to strike the ball with the clubface still descending.

On the tee, the same principles apply, only now the target is the landing area in the fairway. Here's the recipe for helping you reach that landing area. Your eyes track into the landing area. That allows you to aim your clubface down the line on which you want the ball to start. Then you prepare your stance along that line. With a driver, you want to strike the ball with a level or slightly ascending blow, so you adjust your ball position more forward and set your weight more on your right side at address. Use the target line to guide the path of your swing.

So whatever the length of your shot, from the shortest putt to the longest drive, your goal is the target. Your mind should be focused on the target and your swing should react to that target. If that happens, you'll come close to the target more often than not.

There are two steps in this process, and both are critical to success. The first is *visualization* or *target projection*. The second is establishing an efficient preshot routine.

Visualization is the means of creating the reaction to

As you prepare for the shot, your eyes track to the target.

the target. When you swing, you look at the ball, but the ball is not your target. Therefore it is necessary to create a mental image of your actual target, the point where you want the ball to finish. That's only half the battle. Not only do you want to "see" the target in your mind, you want to visualize the flight of the ball in getting to that target.

If you do not get and keep a picture of the target and the path to that target in your mind's eye, you will be swinging only in a general direction. Visualization takes your mind away from the ball and swing mechanics that lock up your mind. It focuses your swing path and instinctively helps you swing the club so it will send the ball in the specific direction you want.

Visualization also calms you mentally so the pace of your swing stays constant and correct. Proper pace demands an ingrained feel for your physical swing and a mental picture of the ball going to the target. Your body then reacts positively to these messages from your mind.

Visualization, along with a good routine, keeps mechanical thoughts from creeping in and forcing you to change the pace of your swing. You may be able to get away with mechanical thoughts for a while, but sooner or later they will catch up with you and cause a bad shot, usually when you want a good one the most.

Your routine starts well before you step up to the ball. We recommend that you begin the preparation for your shot from several paces behind the ball, looking down the line to your target. But however you start, it's vital that you begin the visualization process before the physical process. Before you begin to move into the address position, stand and imagine where you want the ball to end up and how you want it to get there. Fix that image in your mind. The mind conceives and the body receives. It's helpful to talk to yourself. The mind sees in pictures, and words trigger the picture and feel of the proper action. So—under your breath—describe in words the flight of the ball you want and its ultimate destination.

Bruce Crampton, winner of more than 30 tournaments

and more than $4 million on the PGA and Senior PGA Tours, has said that he not only visualizes the flight of the ball but also sees the ball landing on the green, bouncing and rolling to the hole. Jack Nicklaus says he "goes to the movies" and that he never makes a shot, in practice or in competition, without first visualizing the ball on the way to the target and where he wants it to finish.

Your game will improve dramatically if you learn to visualize the target at which you're shooting. So remember that while you're looking at the ball as you address it and swing, your mind's eye should be relating to the target. You should have a vision of the target and the flight of the ball to it as you prepare to make your swing and then actually make it, and you should have an ingrained feeling for the swing that will send the ball to that target. Thus you are preparing your mind, your body and your club at the same time to put the ball into the target area.

Once you get the target and the ball flight fixed in your mind, you must keep it there until you make the swing, without letting in extraneous thoughts. Especially, you must not let those mechanical thoughts interfere. That brings us to routine.

Your preshot routine will be examined in detail in Volume 2 of this series. For now let's discuss what it is and what it does to help you produce better golf shots consistently.

A consistent preshot routine is done in a certain interval of time. It allows you to approach the ball, aim your club, align your body, set yourself, waggle and start the swing the same way every time.

Envision the target and the flight of the ball, which will help you make a swing that sends the ball to that target.

Once you learn to trust your routine—and your swing, of course—you'll find that the start of your swing happens as automatically as possible. You don't have to worry about pulling the trigger.

If you start your swing from a static position, that start often becomes a dreaded moment that few golfers can handle. It disrupts the flow of your swing because invariably your mind will stray to mechanical thoughts and ruin your visualization of the target.

With a good routine, the moment of takeaway becomes no different than any other moment during that routine. The swing will start almost as a reflex, without anxiety and tension. A good routine gives you a feeling for the timing, rhythm and sequence of the swing and puts you in a relaxed state. Once you have practiced and established a routine, you can keep your focus on the target while the swing flows out of that routine.

Did you ever notice what a good practice swing you make, almost every time, when there is no ball in front of you? And when you're actually hitting balls on the practice range, it's relatively easy to develop a relaxed rhythm that produces good shots, because there is no penalty for a bad shot. If you hit it sideways, simply rake over another ball and hit the shot again. It's on the course, where every shot counts, that the tension mounts and the negative thoughts creep in. Taking your practice swing to the golf course is the goal of every player, from the rankest amateur to the best tour professional.

Developing a good, consistent routine can help you do

that. By freeing your mind from the extraneous thoughts, it lets you focus on where you want the ball to go without any worry about the swing that's going to send it there. That being the case, the body won't differentiate between a practice shot on the range or a crucial shot down the stretch in tournament play...or for a $5 nassau with three presses on the line.

2

FEEL STARTS WITH PREPARATION

The primary thought in your mind as your prepare to make a golf shot should be simply the word "swing." You should actually visualize the swinging of the golf club, relating to the grip end and the head end of the club swinging freely to identify the rhythm of motion. To swing with that sense of rhythm and movement, you must stand to the ball properly and you must hold the club correctly.

Holding the Club

The grip is certainly one of the most important elements in an effective golf swing, perhaps the most important. A correct grip insures that the arms are able to swing the club freely on the correct path and the hands can react to square the club-face in the impact area. This is the goal you seek to make good swings and hit good shots. To meet that goal, you must fit your grip—the position of your hands on the club—to your body type, the way you swing and the way you play the game.

There is not one grip that suits every golfer, because hand size and grip strength will vary. The *ideal* grip is the neutral grip, one in which the hands work best together and in which one is not dominant over the other in achieving your goal of free swinging and the squaring of the clubface at the proper time. The neutral grip is one in which the back of the left hand and the palm of the right hand are facing approximately down a line parallel to the target line. To best envision the neutral grip, place your hands together with the fingers extended, as in a praying position. Now lower the hands so they are approximately in the address position. Slide the right hand down until the curve of the right hand thumb pad is just under the curve of the left thumb pad and the two fit snugly together. This is pretty close to the position in which your hands will be when you place them on a golf club.

Remember that the neutral grip is simply the ideal. To accommodate your particular body type and/or swing tendencies, you might have to adjust your grip. We'll elaborate on that later, especially in Volume 2 of this series.

In any case, the hands must be set as close together as possible and must work together as a unit so you have less conflict between the parts of the swing and can create more clubhead speed while maintaining control.

In general, for right-handed players, the grip end or handle of the club should lie in the fingers of the left hand, against the root of the forefinger and running diagonally to a point where it is secured under the heel pad. The left thumb should lie slightly to the right-center of the handle. The right hand should be positioned on the club to allow flexion in the wrists. The handle of the club should fit into the middle two fingers of the right hand. The channel between the thumb and heel pads fits snugly against the left thumb. The thumb and forefinger of the right hand should be set lightly in a trigger position on the club, the right thumb lying on the left side of the handle and forming a V with the forefinger.

Within these parameters there are two basic styles of grip, the Vardon or overlap and the interlocking. In the Vardon grip, named after the famed British player who popularized it, the little finger of the right hand should be laid over the forefinger of the left or hooked around it, laid between the forefinger and the middle finger of the left hand. With the interlocking grip, mainly used by players with small

The handle runs diagonally up underneath the heel pad of the left hand (left). The left thumb sits slightly to the right of center (right).

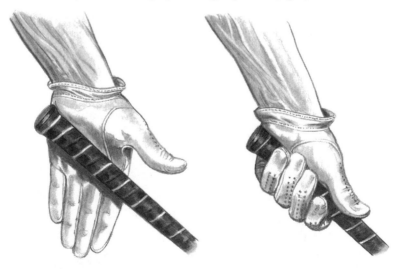

14

hands (Jack Nicklaus and Tom Kite are a couple of examples), the little finger of the right hand is interlocked or entwined with the forefinger of the left.

The other option is the unlap or eight-finger grip, often erroneously referred to as the baseball grip. It is formed exactly the same as the other two except that the little finger of the right is placed on the club rather than hooking over or entwining with the forefinger of the left. This puts the right hand lower on the club in a more dominant position, making it easier to release and square the clubface through impact and to create more clubhead speed.

The grip position will vary, as we said, depending on your body structure, flexibility, physical strength and swing preferences. The neutral or model grip probably is best for

The right thumb and forefinger are in a triggered position (left). *In the Vardon grip* (right), *the little finger of the right hooks around the left forefinger.*

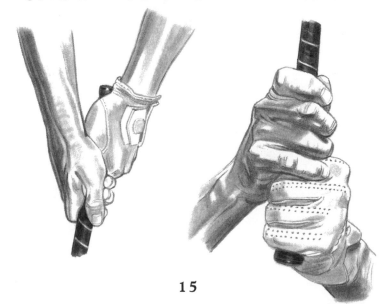

the player of average height or taller with a relatively upright swing. If you are shorter with a swing that goes more around your body, you might want to turn your left hand more to the right to fit that swing. You might want to do the same if you lack strength and need more hand action to create clubhead speed, or if you lack flexibility in your wrists. A weaker player, especially one with small hands, might want to try the unlap grip as a means of increasing clubhead speed. In all cases, the precision with which you put your fingers on the club is extremely important. You must match the bottom line of the club with the shaft angle and the position of your hands to make sure that your fingers and hands will put the clubface in the proper position as you swing through the ball.

The pressure with which you hold the club is extremely

The bottom line of the club must match your hand position.

16

Grip lightly enough to feel the weight of the clubhead.

important, as are the pressure points in your hands. In other words, you must apply pressure in the correct places and in the correct amounts.

The basic guideline is that you apply only as much pressure as you need to control the force of the club throughout your swing. That promotes the flowing motion and rhythm that the good player exhibits. You should be able to feel the weight in the head of the club throughout the swing. Your grip pressure will increase slightly as the length and speed of the swing you are making increases. But it should always be light enough that you are able to feel that head weight as it swings around your body, through the ball and over to the forward side as you finish.

Almost every golfer below the level of professional or top amateur grips the club too tightly. The antidote is to think of gripping the club as lightly as possible, much lighter than you ever imagined. We're not talking loose here. Your grip must remain solid and firm so that the club doesn't slip during the swing. But you can do that while still holding the club lightly, which promotes relaxation in the muscles. The lighter your pressure, the more relaxed your muscles, the faster you can swing. This in turn produces greater distance as well as accuracy.

While technical evidence indicates that grip pressure increases on the backswing and through impact, your thought should be to keep your pressure as constant as possible. The amount of pressure will vary with the club in your hand and the shot you are planning to play. It naturally will be more with the driver than if you are planning a soft pitch shot to the green. But in all cases you should try to keep that pressure constant throughout whatever swing you are making.

Grip pressure should be applied with the last three fingers of each hand, including the little finger of the right. Pressure at these points activates the inside or underneath muscles of the arms, which are the muscles you want to use during the forward swing. This pressure, rather than in the thumbs and forefingers, also eliminates tension and allows a free swinging of the arms.

Applying pressure in the last three fingers only is especially important in the right hand. If the thumb and forefinger get too strongly into the act, which is a common tendency, the right arm is forced higher and the club is likely to be taken back outside and destroy the path and plane of the swing.

If the left arm and side is to lead the swing, a point we will discuss later, you must have more pressure in your left hand than your right. This keeps the right hand from taking control at the change of direction from the top of the swing. There must be some right-hand pressure, of course, to keep the grip stable and help the elbows stay closer together and closer to the body, which is where you want them during the swing. But the pressure should not be as strong as that in the left.

Aiming the Club

Striking the ball to your target with a straight shot is a lot easier if your clubface is pointing to that target. Clubface po-

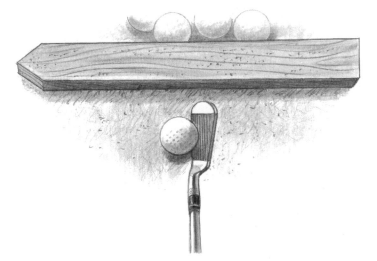

Aim the vertical scoring lines on the face and the leading edge of the club on a track to the target.

sition influences almost everything else in the setup and swing.

Before you aim the club, be sure you hands are on the club in the proper position and in the correct relationship to the clubface. This virtually insures that the clubface will point directly at the target.

We like to use an intermediate target as an aid in aiming the club correctly. It's easier to aim at a spot close to you than at a distant target. Pick out a leaf, a divot or some other spot that is directly on the line between your ball and the target. Then aim your clubface on that spot, using the vertical scoring lines at the heel and toe ends of the clubface. Imagine them as parallel tracks and simply aim that track so it runs directly to the target. This puts the leading edge of your clubface perpendicular to the target line.

Aligning Your Eyes

Because how you see determines how you aim and swing, your eye line should be straight or parallel with your target line and should stay that way throughout the swing. To accomplish this, be sure your head is straight and not tilted to one side or the other. Look at the target by rotating your head to the left rather than lifting it up and around. Just before you start your swing, rotate your chin a bit to the right so that your left eye finds the top of the ball. Keep that position on the backswing and on the forward swing through impact. This keeps your head from moving forward and around as you swing into the ball. It also promotes a sense of the inward and downward path your left arm and club should take from the top into impact. Soon after impact, your eyes and head will turn to the left to watch the flight of the ball.

Practice this, starting on the putting green. There your head and eyes will simply rotate to follow the ball, because it is still on the ground. For shots in the air, your eyes will react to the flight of the ball and your head will come up naturally at the finish of the swing. Incorporate proper eye alignment and head movement and you will take a big step toward aiming and swinging in the right direction.

Aligning Your Body

Once your clubface is aimed, align all parts of your body off that clubface on a line parallel to your target line. Imagine separate lines that run across your toes, knees, hips, shoulders and eyes. If all these lines are parallel to your target line, your body is in the correct alignment.

The common tendency is to aim the body at the target. If you do that, however, the clubface has to be aimed to the right of the target. Instead, your body parts should be aligned parallel left. That's because your body is to the left of the target line. Aligning parallel left creates the illusion that you are set way to the left of your target. Your body may be set just two feet away from the target line, but don't make the mistake of aligning it two feet to the left of your target. At 200 yards, for example, your body should appear to be aimed some 14 yards left of your target.

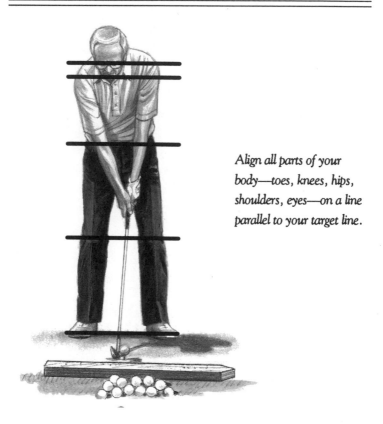

Align all parts of your body—toes, knees, hips, shoulders, eyes—on a line parallel to your target line.

Finding Your Ball Position

It is critical to position your body to the ball so it is in the proper spot in relation to your swing arc, the spot where the club will come into the ball at the best possible angle.

With the irons and fairway woods you want to strike the ball with a slightly descending blow. With the driver and the ball on a tee, you want to catch the ball after the club has reached the bottom of its arc and is slightly on the upswing.

You'll want to experiment with ball position, because it depends on your type of swing and the strength of your lower-body action. Our experience has been that almost every amateur should play the ball more toward the center of the stance. In general, with the driver the ball should be played from just off the left instep or left heel to a couple of inches back of the heel. With the fairway woods, position the ball just ahead of center in your stance. With the irons, start with the ball in the center of your stance, then adjust, depending on what is happening with your shots. If the ball is starting too far right or is hooking too much, move it forward until you get the shot shape you're looking for.

Posture — Standing to the Ball

Correct posture will help you swing the club the way you want to. If you stand correctly to the ball, you won't get in your own way and will be able to make a free arm swing that takes the club back and through on the correct path and plane.

Our guidelines for the posture at address that will promote this freedom in the arms are as follows:

1. Your weight usually should be set more on the right side than on the left. When you put your right hand lower than your left on the club, it naturally moves your weight more to the right, so this becomes the natural position. Setting your weight on the right side helps the hips and shoulders turn easily. It promotes the shifting of the weight farther to the right and allows the arms to swing freely around and up, supported by the legs, on the backswing. There are variations dictated by your intended angle of approach into the ball, and this is especially true for the short shots, but in general the guideline should be that the farther you are trying to hit the ball, the more your weight should be on the right side at address.

At address, your knees should be slightly flexed, your back straight but tilted from the hips, your arms hanging from your relaxed shoulders.

2. Your weight should be toward the balls of your feet. We didn't say on your toes. We said more toward the balls of the feet than the heels. This induces a feeling of catlike mobility in your lower body, a readiness to turn and shift, promoting the good leg movement that supplements a free motion in your swing.

3. In general, the knees should be slightly flexed, only enough to unlock them and no more than three or four inches. But that might not work for everybody, especially taller players who might need to flex their knees a bit more. George Archer is a prime example. No matter how much you flex your knees, the key is to tilt your upper body properly, which will happen as a reaction to looking downward at the ball, and to keep your weight toward the balls of the feet. This will induce a springy tension in the insides of your legs and the backs of your thighs. If you let your weight at address go to the heels, your back is forced into a position that is too erect, placing more pressure on your spine and creating more tension in your back. Your ability to turn properly also will be inhibited.

4. Your back should be straight but tilted forward from the hips so that the arms hang freely suspended from the shoulders. Create a small amount of tension in the small of your back to keep it straight. Stick out your buttocks slightly. Keep your head erect, in line with the spine. Make sure that while your spine is straight, it is tilted forward enough that the arms hang freely. Your arms and the club shaft should not be in a straight line. There should be a definite angle there.

This posture position encourages that free swinging of the arms and a natural turning of the upper body.

5. Set your right side lower than your left, your knees cocked slightly to the left. Just as the right hand positioned below the left moves your weight naturally to the right side, it also sets your entire right side slightly lower than the left. Your right side should feel soft and "broken" at address, which allows it to turn easily out of the way on the backswing. To further this position, cock your knees to the left (being sure to do

Your right side should be lower than your left and feel soft and "broken," your knees cocked slightly to the target.

so on a line parallel to the target line), which makes the right leg a firmer support for your backswing.

The width of the stance is an individual thing that varies with a player's physical stature and flexibility, which in turn govern the ability to make an unrestricted pivot. The thinner, more flexible player can use a wider stance. A stockier player who is less flexible may have to play from a narrower stance to maintain his free arm swing. The rule is that your stance should be as wide as possible to give you a stable foundation but not so wide that it inhibits a free arm swing and body turn.

3

THE GOLF SWING—A PHILOSOPHY

Considering the task at hand, the nature of the game, the need to propel a small ball varying distances to a target of varying sizes, the golf swing is one of the most intricate motions in all of sport.

At the same time, it can and should be one of the easiest and most graceful motions.

The golf swing is made up of a seemingly complex number of parts, a series of movements. If the movements are correct and in their proper sequence, the swing has a chance to be correct. In the following chapters we're going to examine how those parts work and the roles they play in an effective swing. We'll break down the parts as follows: the first swing—hands, wrists and forearms; the second swing—arms swinging freely from the shoulders; the pivot—the role of the feet, legs and torso. In the final chapter we'll put all those parts together and give you an explanation and discussion of the *whole* swing.

We can't stress enough that the last is the most important chapter of all. No swing can be done efficiently and effectively with part thoughts. The parts must be learned, of course. You will need conceptual understanding and, frankly, a lot of practice to get the parts working well. But then those parts must be incorporated into a whole swing, and the feel of that swing must be ingrained into the mind and muscles of the player. You cannot play well if you are thinking about mechanical motions. You need a total picture that will develop the feel of the entire swing. That will send the ball to your target.

But the swing only works well if it is properly timed, and herein lies the problem for the majority of golfers. They do not have the knowledge or the understanding of what it takes to propel a golf ball forward in the most efficient manner.

To properly time your golf swing, you must swing at a pace that is right for you. Most of you don't do that. You equate distance with speed, and you equate speed with effort. So you succumb to the "hit impulse" and try to bash the ball as hard as you can, which totally destroys the pace of your swing and any sense of timing.

Clubhead speed is important, of course. Ultimately, it determines how far you can strike the ball. In golf, speed is power. But there are two overriding considerations involved here.

The first and most important is that you must produce on-center contact, a square hit with the clubface square to the target line and going straight down the path to the target at impact. You can swing the club at 100 miles an hour or more, but if you don't achieve these elements, the shot will go off line and not as far as it should.

The second is the element that produces clubhead speed in the first place. Speed does not equate with effort. If you think it does, try consciously swinging as hard as you can. Your muscles will tighten and your swing will actually slow down. Conversely, try swinging slowly with your muscles relaxed. See how much better chance you have of making on-center contact, how much faster your swing will be and how much farther the ball will travel. It also will go a lot straighter.

Most golfers are power-oriented, but they don't know how to apply the power they have, so they waste most of it. The amount of effort that goes into a swing is not nearly as important as how that power is applied. The three factors that produce power, which in turn produces longer shots, are strength, speed and flexibility. Strength is not nearly as important as the other two. If it were, slender little guys like Chi Chi Rodriguez and Bob Toski could not hit the ball nearly as far as they do. Clubhead speed is a product of flexibility and proper timing throughout the swing. Even a bomber like John Daly, who is obviously strong, is generating his speed with an overly long swing that is the result of flexibility. And certainly it requires good timing. He is not going at the ball with brute force. He stays nicely in balance from start through the finish, which means he is swinging with control at all times.

The speed of your swing is a reaction to the distance you want the ball to go. Your speed on a tee shot will be greater than your speed on a putt. But you should not make any conscious effort to make one faster than the other. The speed of a particular shot is greater because the swing is longer. If your swing is properly timed, the length of the swing and the centrifugal force acting on the clubhead will increase the speed coming through the ball.

The swing should be made in a leisurely manner, both going back and coming through. Take it away in leisurely fashion and start it down from the top the same way.

It doesn't require great physical effort to swing a club that weighs less than a pound and strike a ball that weighs less than two ounces. Don't let the hit impulse jump in. Don't overexert yourself when you don't have to. A well-timed swing comes from a controlled motion of the arms and body.

What does "leisurely" mean? What is too fast and what is too slow? Seldom do we see a player swing the club back and down too slowly. If you swing the club back so slowly that you have no sense of motion, no feeling of rhythm and flow in the swing, you're swinging too slowly. But that's rare. On the other hand, we see thousands who swing it too fast, and there is a simple guideline to determine if your swing pace is too quick—you can swing the club with control only as fast as the strength of your hands and forearms can bear.

If you are to strike the ball squarely with consistency, you must control the force of the swinging club. If you take the club back too quickly or start it down too quickly, the speed of your swing and the weight of the club will cause you to lose control. You will have to compensate with some hand and/or body action that will throw your swing out of sequence.

There should be a feeling of ease as you swing the club back and change direction at the top into the forward swing.

Never feel that you are swinging the club hard. If you don't feel at ease during the swing, you have swung too fast and are going out of control. Your muscles will tighten and you are heading for trouble.

Don't worry about generating speed through impact. You instinctively will want to swing at the ball hard and fast. Your problem is to control the pace of the swing through the backswing and the critical change of direction. If you can do that, speed at impact will come naturally. It also will be more effective speed, because you will have a much greater chance of striking the ball squarely with the center of the face.

So your own strength and coordination should determine the pace of your swing, with control always being the determining factor.

A warning here—you should not *overcontrol* the swing. There must always be *motion*, a rhythm and flow to your swing that lets you generate clubhead speed effortlessly. If your swing is stilted or contrived in an attempt to achieve maximum control, your muscles will tighten and you will lose the distance and accuracy you seek.

You must feel the force of the swing. Try this exercise: with your arm outstretched, hold a club lightly with your thumb and forefinger. Start it swinging back and forth and just let it swing, feeling the motion as it goes to and fro. Notice how it comes to a gradual and gentle halt as it swings back, then gradually swings forward again, then back again. That's the feeling you want to have in your swing, when you have both hands on the club and are utilizing all your body parts. The swing is back and forth, smooth and effortless, all

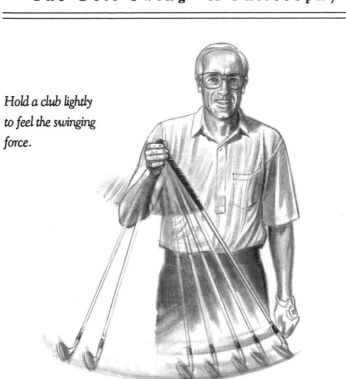

Hold a club lightly to feel the swinging force.

the while feeling the clubhead and the gradual buildup of force in that swing. You must develop a feel for the swinging force with the movements of the body complementing that force, all the parts of the body moving in the proper sequence and speed in conjunction with the swinging of the arms, hands and club. We'll deal with the movement of the body in Chapter Six. For now, just be aware that it supports the swinging of the arms.

The feel for the swinging force of the club starts in the hands and arms and the feet. Your hands and arms control the swinging of the club around your body, and the movement of your feet controls the lower body as it supports the movement of the upper body.

We believe that the essence of the swing lies in the movement of the hands and arms, with the body supporting, and not the other way around. Most players who try to control the swing with the big muscles of the body will lose distance, as well as accuracy, simply because big muscles do not move as fast as small muscles. You cannot move your hips or your shoulders as fast as you can move your arms. And you cannot swing your arms as fast as you can flap your hands. Therefore, it stands to reason that if you can time the movement of the faster muscles in your hands and arms, you can produce greater clubhead speed and thus more distance.

We've heard good players say that when they want to hit the ball farther they drive their legs harder and faster. We contend that a faster and harder leg drive is simply a subconscious reaction to the fact that they know they will be swinging their arms faster to get greater distance. Instinctively, they will move their legs faster to support that faster arm swing.

You do not strike the ball with your legs. You strike the ball with the swinging of your hands and arms. The legs and torso just move to support that swinging motion.

In any case, you must feel the swing throughout. Learn to acquire awareness by developing a feel for when a movement is correct or incorrect. Let your mind identify where the club is during the swing instead of consciously trying to direct it to a certain position. We learn through mistakes. In other words, we must feel that the club is out of position before we can correct the swing error.

Which brings us right back to light grip pressure and lack of tension in the muscles. Minimal grip pressure and relaxed muscles not only allow more flexibility and subsequently more clubhead speed, it also allows you much better touch in making any golf shot, from a drive to a putt. The more touch you have, the better you are able to find the golf ball with the face of the club, striking it squarely and accurately.

Touch and feel help eliminate the hit impulse and promote the swing impulse. They help you develop a sense of swinging *through* the ball rather than at it, a feeling that the ball simply gets in the way as the club passes through the impact area.

Once you have trained your mind and muscles to reach that point, then you are ready to play golf.

4

THE FIRST SWING—
HANDS, WRISTS AND
FOREARMS

The golf swing is a system of levers. In the full swing, there actually are three of these levers, the left arm being the first, the club and the hands being the second and the body the third. But for practical purposes, you should be concerned about only the first two.

A lever transmits force or motion. The purpose in the full swing is to create enough motion in the second lever—the hands and club—to transmit as much force as possible to the ball. Thus you must have enough motion in the first lever, your left arm, and allow the second lever to work about its hinge—the wrist—to increase that motion and create greater speed.

The flail-like action of the second lever working off the first lever produces maximum clubhead speed. If you didn't cock your wrists during the backswing, you would be going with just one lever, so you could not generate nearly as much speed. The levering action of the club is created by the application of physical force that causes a buildup of momentum in the clubhead as it swings. That's true whether you are creating the second lever on your backswing or releasing it on your forward swing.

If you have done everything else correctly in the backswing and early stages of the forward swing, you really don't have to worry about the action of the all-important second lever. It will work efficiently without your having to think about it.

The first swing, then, is the action of the hands, wrists and forearms as they swing the golf club. Let's define their responsibilities.

The hands basically will cock, uncock and recock through the swing. As you swing back, the left hand pushes downward while the right hand pulls upward to cock the club. On the forward swing your hands will uncock until they are basically in the starting position at impact, then will recock through impact. Your wrists give you the flexibility to allow that to happen.

Let's first examine that cocking action of the hands on the backswing. *When* you cock your hands going back is a matter of personal preference that depends on your physical strength and agility. The earlier you begin that cocking action, setting the angle between your left arm and the clubshaft, the better off you are. But "early" does not mean "quickly." The motivating force in your backswing must be a smooth, rhythmic arm swing, so the cocking of your hands should be done slowly and smoothly in conjunction with that swing. This swinging of your left arm creates the momentum that causes a weight buildup in the clubhead as you come to the top of your swing. This in turn will cause your

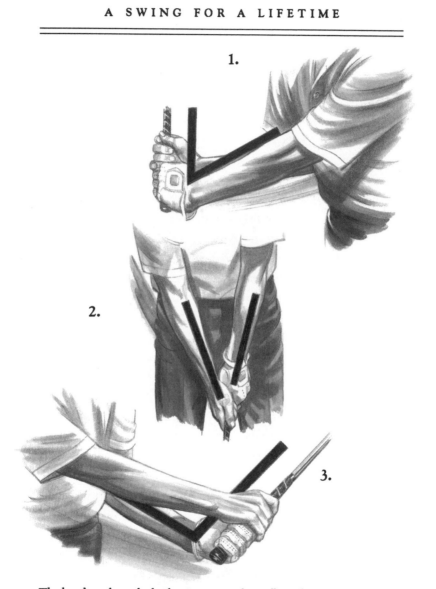

1.

2.

3.

The hands cock on the backswing, return basically to the starting position at impact, then recock following through.

hands to finish cocking automatically if you don't do anything to interfere with that action.

How do the hands cock starting back? You don't flap or hinge them in one direction or the other. Simply cock them so the thumbs stay in basically the same relationship with the forearms that they were in at address. To get a feel for the movement, take your normal grip and address position with any club. Then, without moving your arms, pick the club straight up with your hands until the shaft is approximately parallel to the ground and is pointing straight in front of you. That's the correct cocking of your hands.

By concentrating your grip pressure in the last three fingers of the left hand and maintaining control in those fingers as you start back, you encourage the hands to begin cocking immediately without a lot of conscious effort. By the time you reach the top of your swing, they will be completely cocked. But that will only happen if your grip pressure is light enough so you can feel the weight of the clubhead going back and instinctively cock it into position. That light grip pressure also lets the left arm swing freely going back so the momentum of the club is the dominant factor. If your grip is too tight, none of that will happen.

Now let's look at what the forearms do. First try it without a club. Stretch your arms out in front of you in the address position, hands together, as if you were going to shake hands with the ball. Then simply extend your thumbs. As your arms swing halfway back, about waist high, they rotate in a clockwise direction and your right arm folds. This allows your thumbs to go into an upward position. When you swing

The forearms first rotate clockwise, then counterclockwise.

down, your forearms rotate counterclockwise back to the impact position, where the thumbs basically point at the ball. On the follow-through, your forearms continue to rotate, the left arm folds, and when the arms get to about waist high again your thumbs once more will point straight up. Through it all, your arms are rotating and swinging freely from side to side.

Now, with a club in your hands and a ball on a tee in front of you, combine those two movements: the swinging of your forearms and the cocking of your hands. Don't try for distance—simply make a little tapping motion through the ball. Swing your hands and forearms back. You will feel that as you swing back your right elbow will fold while your hands are cocking. As you swing through, you will feel your hands uncock, squaring the clubface through impact, then recock. Your left elbow will fold on the follow-through. So the motion is swinging and cocking, swinging and uncocking and recocking. Because your hands and wrists are your greatest speed producers, you will find that you can strike your golf ball a considerable distance with minimal effort. Let's say you normally hit a 6-iron about 150 yards. You can get about 40 percent of that distance with the simple little motion we've just described.

And that motion is the heartbeat of the golf swing. It helps you sense the feeling of the weight in the head of the club as it swings back and in and around, then down and through the ball.

The job of your hands, wrists and forearms is to create speed through flexibility and motion and to square the clubface at impact. Which brings us to the point we have repeatedly made before. Most golfers wanting distance—and we all do—relate it to power and effort. But that doesn't get it. Distance comes from clubhead speed and centerface contact. You don't need a lot of effort. You need flexibility and freedom, sensitivity and feel, in swinging the club. That's what produces distance.

DRILLS

Tee to Retee Drill

Put a tee in the hole at the end of the handle of your club. Grip down on the club so you can comfortably feel the weight in the head. Then swing the club back just far enough

that your wrists cock and the tee in the end of the shaft is
pointing at the ball. Now swing the club down and through
so that on the follow-through the tee is pointing to where
the ball was. This may be the primary drill for developing
sensitivity in swinging the club and identifying the feeling of
squaring up the clubface and getting maximum speed with
the least possible effort.

The Chair Drill

This is a drill that emphasizes the use of your hands. It looks
difficult, but it really isn't, and it's a lot of fun. You need a 3-
wood with the ball on a tee and a folding chair or other chair
without any arms. Position the chair so you can sit on the
right front corner. Set your right leg so it almost feels as if it's
behind you and feel you are reaching slightly for the ball at

address. Grip down on the club a little bit for better control. Pretend you are driving your car. You are going to strap yourself in with your seat belt so you can't jump around. Hold the club lightly enough that you can feel the weight in the head. Now, using just your hands, wrists and forearms, merely swing the club around and behind you, then back and through the ball. Just let the club swing and find the golf ball. At the finish of the swing you should still be facing the tee in the ground, which indicates that you used a maximum amount of action with the hands, wrists and forearms and a minimum amount of body action. You will be surprised, probably amazed, at how far you can strike the golf ball with that minimal amount of effort.

Incidentally, go off to the end of the range or away from other practicers when you first try this drill. That's so there will be no accidents until you learn how to do it.

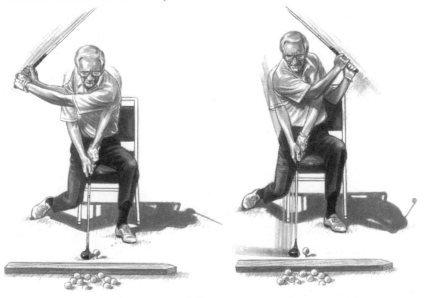

5

THE SECOND SWING— ARMS SWINGING FREELY FROM THE SHOULDERS

The second swing is the swinging of the arms freely from the shoulders—not with the shoulders, mind you, but the upper arms swinging freely from the shoulders.

This actually is a continuation of the lever system we discussed in Chapter Four. The so-called first lever, the left arm, actually swings from the torso, specifically the shoulder. But the torso simply serves as a base, a support, for the arms in the golf swing. We will examine that more closely in the next two chapters, but that's all its job really is.

The free swinging of the upper arms from the shoulders adds length to the swing and gives you a full motion. If you try to make your shoulders control the swing, you end up with something that is very tight and tense and produces very little speed, let alone solid contact. The shoulders simply assist as carriers of the hands and arms. The swinging of the club with the hands and arms will turn the shoulders freely and create all the clubhead speed you need. The faster

*The free swinging
of the arms gives
you a full motion.*

the arms swing, the faster the shoulders will turn. A turn will not create a swing, but a swing will create a turn.

So, while the hands and wrists are still cocking, add the second component of the golf swing by swinging the arms back farther. The purpose of the second swing is to transport the hands, wrists and forearms and to give your motion a sense of rhythm and freedom. Now your arms are swinging about 180 degrees going back and about 180 degrees going through, but your shoulders are turning only about 90 degrees each way. Your body turns, but it's in response to the swing.

How does this swinging of the arms support the cocking and particularly the uncocking of the hands? This is important, because, having cocked the hands going back to create the second lever, we have to apply that force most effectively.

Swinging the arms, and particularly the left arm, forward along the proper path will accomplish that. It's a flail-like action, and you don't need to worry about any independent movement of the hands.

We've heard good players over the years say they hit with their hands at impact. We believe that what they are feeling is the response of their hands, particularly the right hand, to the buildup of centrifugal force. Scientific research tells us that if the centrifugal forces are allowed to build properly in the forward swing, by the time you get to impact the clubhead is moving so fast that all your hands can do is hang on. You cannot manipulate them independently at that point.

So, once you have trained your hands to remain passive, they are simply catching up, reacting to the swinging of the arms and uncocking to square the clubface at impact.

The forward swing only requires .2 to .25 of a second, which is just about the time it takes the brain to receive an external signal and relay it to the muscles for appropriate action. Therefore it is almost impossible to make any adjustment in your forward swing once it has started. Scientific tests have proved that once a player is barely into the forward swing he is totally committed to that swing and cannot do anything to change it.

Centrifugal force, if you combine correct swing positions with a light grip pressure that reduces tension, not only will produce great clubhead speed but will also let the hands square the clubface naturally at impact, which means you'll hit the ball longer and straighter, too. It will do that *if we don't do anything to interfere with it.* Unfortunately, we usually do. In an effort to get more power and distance, we instinctively try to do so with brute strength. We tighten our grip on the club, lunge with the shoulders or cast with the hands at the wrong time, thus destroying our timing and the effortless buildup of power that centrifugal force creates.

There may be a need in certain types of players to develop better hand action—weaker players, shorter, stockier players who swing more around their body, players who have for one reason or other sublimated their hands and need more hand speed in their swings. If this is the case with you, you may have to train your hands so they can work naturally, as contradictory as that sounds. It will take some practice and some time before you can make it work consistently on the course, but you must develop hand action that blends with a good arm swing and the support of the lower body and comes into play at the correct time. Teach your hands to work properly so they won't jump in at the wrong time and interfere with the natural action of the lever system.

Then you can allow the second swing—the swinging of the arms freely from the shoulders—to effectively unleash the power of centrifugal force. Remember, when you do this you are not swinging the golf club harder or more powerfully. You are simply swinging it longer and more freely. And suddenly this second component of the swing has added about 60 yards to your distance. Now your 6-iron is going considerably farther without any appreciable increase in effort.

DRILLS

Feet-Together Drill

Assume your normal address position, then bring your right foot in next to your left so your feet are together. It's a good idea, as in all these drills, to put the ball on a tee. Then swing. You'll find that your body effort is diminished but the swinging motion of your hands and arms is increased and is more effortless at the same time. And the distance you get will surprise you. This is the feeling you want to have. If your body effort becomes too violent with your feet together, you will fall down.

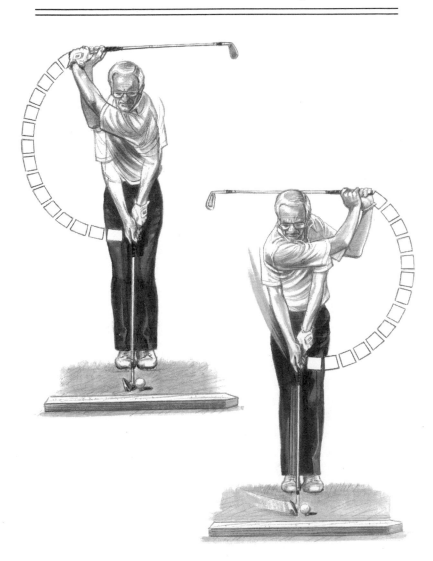

Back-to-Target Drill

This is a drill for those of you who tend to slice the ball because your shoulders will not allow your arms to swing freely past your body, with the clubhead releasing and squaring up through impact.

To do this drill, take your regular starting position. Locate your left shoulder as your focal point, then turn your feet and body 90 degrees so your back is to the target. Now turn your hands, arms and club so you address the ball. You still want to sense and feel the club swinging on your regular path to hit the ball to the target—behind you and up on the backswing, then down and through, striking the ball and swinging over to the finish. You should feel that you are letting the club release and going right on past your body. (This is another drill to do away from the crowd until you get the hang of it.)

The purpose of this drill is to create arm rotation and get the feeling that your arms and hands are swinging the club down without your body interfering and turning past the ball, which tends to make the grip end get way ahead of the clubhead and results in your slicing the ball to the right. Because your body already is turned 90 degrees away from the ball, you have to swing your arms and hands freely to make solid contact on the right path. Your body can't interfere.

That's the feeling you want to have when you swing from a normal address position.

1.

2. →

3.

6

THE PIVOT—FEET, LEGS AND TORSO

Now you are ready to add the third component to your swing—the pivot, the movement of the feet, legs and torso that supports the two swings.

The pivot is a result of your arm swing, and the length of your arm swing is a reaction to the distance you want to strike the ball. If you have a driver in your hand and want to hit the ball only five feet, you will simply tap the ball with your hands. There will be no pivot. If you want to drive the ball 250 yards, you will make a full swing and pivot. You need time and leverage to hit the ball that far, and the pivot helps provide that.

Think about the times you've had an extremely long putt and said afterward that you had pivoted on it. You didn't try to pivot. It was just that your arm swing had to be so long to roll the ball that far that your body was pulled to the right and back to the left.

When we watch a really good player, we see that the

body turns in harmony with the swinging of the arms and the club. He senses how fast he should move his body related to what the club is doing. A properly paced arm-and-hand swing gives his body time to respond to that motion. The legs follow the swinging of the arms going back and are put into position to lead the forward swing, accommodating the movement of the upper body and arms and putting them in position to accelerate the club properly through the ball. Good players allow the pivot to happen.

Less effective players try to make the body move the club. Instead of relating to a gradual increase in arm speed as they start back down, they react to the power urge by spinning their shoulders or otherwise making an effort with the upper body that disrupts the sequence of hand, arm and body movement and ruins the shot. There is no question that the overuse of shoulders or hips, or both, is the No. 1 cause of inconsistency in the golf swing.

So relate the length of your arm swing to the distance you want to strike the ball and let that control your pivot and your swing.

Don't get the idea that the pivot, the proper action of feet and legs, happens automatically. It does not, and if you think it does, your arms are likely to run off and leave your feet fixed in a static position. It is not a jerky, step-by-step sequence but rather a smooth flow of motion that happens early enough in the backswing to give your arms the freedom to swing.

Many players, in fact, need to work consciously on the movement of their feet and legs to support the swinging of the arms back and through. This is not contradictory to our declaration that the arms lead and the body follows. That's what happens in the ideal swing, but the feet and legs often have to be trained to join in the movement rather than resisting it.

How exactly does the pivot work? To feel the movement in its rawest form, spread your feet into your normal address position and fold your arms behind your back. Then simply move your feet, legs and hips back and forward, back and forward, all the while staying light on your feet. It works from the ground up—the movement of the feet turns

Practice without a club to feel the footwork and pivot.

the knees, the knees turn the hips.

Let's look at it more closely. On the turn back, the left foot rolls and turns inward, the heel coming up as the left knee swings inward and ends up pointing to the right of the ball, while the right hip turns clockwise out of the way. Most of the weight you had on your left side moves from the outside of the left foot to the inside of the right foot. On the forward swing, the left heel goes down, the weight moves from the right foot to the inside and then to the outside of the left foot. The knees help shift the weight forward while the hips turn in a counterclockwise manner.

The action of the knees, individually and together, is important. You hear a lot about turning your hips quickly and clearing your left side on the forward swing. This does happen, but the problem is that thinking in that direction usually causes you to spin your hips too quickly, stiffening your left leg too soon and throwing your upper body out and around. Instead, you should feel that from the top of the backswing the knees first move laterally, then around. At impact, the left knee should be the part of your body farthest forward or closest to the target.

Specifically, the left knee moves laterally to control the vertical and rotary movements at the start of the backswing, while the right knee is responsible for the rotary dimension of the swing. The movement of the left knee toward the target gets the lower body going laterally, while the pushing off the inside of the right foot, which causes the pushing of the right knee, eventually forces the left knee to rotate. This causes the hips and upper body to turn and the left knee to stiffen, but it all happens in the proper sequence. As the left knee starts, the right knee reacts and moves toward the target. That gets your weight off your right leg and supports the motion of your arms swinging forward. It is a coordinated movement. Just move backward and forward in your swing and try to strike the ball with the club coming on a path from inside your target line. With practice, your feet, knees and hips will move correctly . . . if you don't do anything to interfere with the movement. Sense the movements . . . don't force them.

Now put this movement together with the swinging of the hands, arms and club. As you go through your routine and get ready to start the club back, your hands are feeling the club and your feet are feeling the ground—in both cases lightly and in relaxed motion. Your hands and feet momentarily come to a stop, but the movement goes to the knees, which cock slightly forward, parallel to the target line, the instant before you take the club back. The feet and legs turn and move to support the swinging of the arms and in harmony with that swinging as the right hip turns away. This allows your arms to stay flexible and feel the club as it swings. A good thought, both starting back and starting forward, is that your left foot and knee are tied to the swinging of your left hand and arm.

On the forward swing, the feet and knees reverse the motion as the arms swing down, the left knee moving laterally, the right knee pushing forward and the left hip turning out of the way to help the arms swing freely past the body on the correct path.

All this may not happen exactly at the same time. The hands and arms may start slightly sooner on the backswing because they have farther to travel than the lower body, a subject we'll discuss in Chapter Seven. The feet and knees may initiate the forward swing even before the arms and hands have finished going back, especially in a good player, so they can be in position to support the arms swinging down. Because they are heavier and slower muscles, they need a head start. In each case, one movement is in response to the other, but the movements happen smoothly and harmoniously and in the correct sequence. The lower body doesn't get ahead of the arms on the backswing, and the arms and shoulders don't move ahead of the lower body coming forward. It's the proper blend at the proper time that makes an efficient and effective swing.

To sum up, the purpose of the pivot is to provide the weight shift and support for the swinging of your hands and arms. The feet and knees turn the hips to give you agility and freedom, while the swinging of the hands and arms turns the shoulders. The three basic moves in golf are swing, turn and shift. Synchronizing those movements gives you the feel for swinging a golf club and develops balance, speed and solid ball contact.

Remember, the club is the big deal. It must be swung. The body moves to allow that to happen. All that does is help you hit it far and straight.

Step-In Drill

1.

2.

3.

DRILLS

Step-In Drill

This is the first drill we recommend to help you develop proficiency with your weight shift. Tee your ball slightly off the ground. Take your regular starting position. Then move your left foot over to your right foot. Move the clubhead to your right, so it's positioned in front of your eyes. If you leave the club behind the ball, your shoulders will swing open and throw you out of position.

Next, swing and turn freely to the top. From the top, step into the ball with your left foot as if you were swinging at a baseball, then feel your arms swing forward and through the ball into the finish position.

This helps develop the sense of moving your feet and legs laterally to support the swinging of your hands and arms.

The Machine Gun Drill

This is a fun drill and one that is very effective in sensing the movements of your body, with each part contributing its fair share. Its purpose is to develop the harmony between the movement of the feet and legs and the swinging of the hands, arms and club.

Tee up five balls in a row, slightly off the ground, as shown. Take a few practice swings to begin to sense the free movement of your arms and body, then start walking and swinging, walking and swinging, striking each ball without

stopping as the parts of your body move freely to support the swinging of the club.

This drill and all the other drills are fun. Do them daily, even if it's at home in your back yard with a plastic ball. They increase your sensitivity for swinging the club, and that's what we're after.

7

THE WHOLE SWING—
PUTTING IT ALL
TOGETHER

Let's now put everything together. The cocking of the hands and the forearms swinging the club delivers about 40 percent of the distance you can hit a golf ball. By adding the upper arms swinging freely from the shoulders, you add about another 40 percent. Now you have two of the three elements. You have the two swings—the swinging of the club and the swinging of the arms.

Finally you add the pivot to support and time those two swings, and you have 100 percent efficiency without a lot of effort—and, by the way, that's what *swing* means.

The swinging of the club and the swinging of the arms supported by the pivot gives your swing a vertical, a lateral and a rotary dimension that fits your body type and fits your needs depending on which club you have in your hand.

The hands are largely responsible for the vertical dimension of your swing—they swing the club *up*. The arms and legs are largely responsible for the lateral dimension—

The hands swing the club up in the vertical dimension.

*The arms and legs swing the club from side to side laterally (1 and 2),
while the shoulders and hips (3 and 4) add the rotary dimension.*

they move the club *from side to side*. Your shoulders and hips are responsible for the rotary motion—they turn the club *around* your body.

These motions need to be done in a sequence that fits your needs. We like to see some individuals perhaps start the swing with their hands cocking. Others we like to see start the swing with their arms moving first. Still others, depending on the nature of their bodies and particular needs, should start with the hips turning first.

Whatever method fits you best, always remember that the big deal is to learn to swing the club and get an on-time release.

Within the basic parameters of the golf swing—the two swings supported by the body—there are elements that make that swing work repeatedly and effectively. These are factors that you must be aware of. You will have to think about them and practice them and incorporate them into the basic swing. Further, you must "internalize" the feel of these elements into a feel for the whole swing, so that when you go on the golf course and try to make a score, you won't have to be worrying about the parts of your swing. All you want to be concerned about then is making the shot required, sending the ball where you want it to go and getting it in the hole in the fewest number of strokes possible.

The basis of our swing concept is really quite simple: the lead arm and side control the swing, the arms and legs control the body, it's essential to have a feel for the swing and, finally, pace is the factor that lets you put it all together.

The Left Side is the Leader

Let's examine the role of the left side (in right-handers, of course) as the leader in the golf swing. Golf is neither a left-sided nor a right-sided game. It is a two-sided, two-handed game. But the leading hand, arm and side must control the movement of the right or trailing side, no matter how fast that side moves.

So the left side is the leader, the right side the follower. If the left side doesn't lead the swing of a right-handed player, the right arm (and usually the right shoulder) will take over, because that side is stronger and more coordinated. You instinctively want to get it into the act. That's fine in most activities—tennis, bowling, throwing an object or even writing your name. But golf is a bilateral sport in which both sides play vital roles in producing the leverage needed to play the game well.

Go back to our discussion of centrifugal force, which is defined as a force that impels something *outward* from a center of rotation—in this case, the clubhead swinging outward around the body. The opposite of that is *centripetal* force, which tends to pull inward toward a center of rotation. It is the centripetal force or inward pulling that harnesses the centrifugal force and lets it work effectively in the golf swing. There must be a counterbalancing pulling force to harnesses the outward swinging force of the clubhead. In essence, for purposes of the golf swing, centrifugal force is created by a pulling action.

Also, you can pull something straighter than you can push it, especially when there is a hinge involved, as there is in a two-lever golf swing. Anybody who has ever pushed or pulled a child's wagon would agree.

You pull with your left or lead side because it is in front of the shaft and clubhead from takeaway through impact. You push with your right side, because it is behind the shaft. So the only way you can maintain a pulling force through impact is to keep your power source, the left arm, ahead of the object you're pulling, which is the club. If you begin to push too soon with your right side, especially the right arm or upper body, and use physical force to operate the second lever, you will tend to force open the angle between your left arm and the clubshaft and will dissipate its force too early. You also will tend to force the clubhead off the correct path and the clubface out of position. If the right arm begins to dominate and breaks down the left, it cannot move *through* the left. It must move out and around.

Again, we're not talking one-sided here. The right side plays a vital role in adding feel, speed and power to the swing. Through the early stages of the forward swing the right arm itself is helping pull the club as long as it stays ahead of the shaft and head. And in the impact area the right arm and hand begin to push to add extra power.

But that push is a reaction to pull. The right side works well only as long as it's in harmony with the left. Many good players talk about hitting with the right side, but they can do this only because the left remains in control.

So, if you're not a tour-caliber player yet, you should try for the feeling of swinging the left arm inward and downward to allow the clubhead to release properly. It's instinctive to find the ball with the right hand and arm. To play well, you must learn to find it with your left.

Left-side control begins at the start of the swing. You will tend to control the forward swing with the side that controlled the backswing. On the backswing the right arm simply supports the left, staying relaxed and letting the left arm set the pace. If the right arm gets tight, it tends to shorten the backswing, cutting off the backward motion and forcing you too quickly into the forward swing.

When the club gets to the top, the weight of the club-head and the speed at which it's moving puts a lot of pressure on the handle end. Therefore, when the club is started back down, it's necessary to exert more pressure with the left hand, simply because it's closer to the handle end than the right. That's difficult, maybe impossible, to do if the left hand is not in control going back.

Hit a lot of "fat" shots, the club striking the ground behind the ball? That's because you have little control with the left side while the right side dominates. This causes the wrists to uncock too early in the forward swing, moving away from the body instead of moving in close to it as you swing through impact.

You can overcome that and other shortcomings by programming your left side to control the club before you step up to the shot. Then, by aiming your clubface and aligning your body properly, you can swing the golf club on the correct path and will begin to experience the left arm moving left after impact and controlling the force of the right.

The Path Is Inside to Inside

If you want to hit the ball straight, or reasonably so, the club-head must be traveling down the target line—or the line on which you want your ball to start—at impact. However, the clubhead cannot remain on the target line throughout the swing. You'd have to swing like a Ferris wheel turns, a physical impossibility.

The ideal path of the clubhead on the forward swing is *from inside the target line to down the line to back inside*. To prove this, hold a club in front of you, parallel to the ground, and swing it as if it were a baseball bat. The clubhead will swing immediately inside the line going back, returning from inside to on the line at the point of impact, then swinging immediately back inside the line on the follow-through. Because the swing is horizontal, the clubhead is on the target just for an instant.

Now set the club on the ground in your normal address position. Because the plane of the club (another element we'll talk about in a moment) is now more vertical, your clubhead can stay on the line a bit longer. But you still are swinging more or less around your body, so the clubhead follows generally the same inside-to-inside path on the forward swing.

The good player is instinctively aware of the path of his swing directed along the target line. The higher handicapper, unfortunately, usually is not. The majority of amateurs swing too much to the left, from outside the target line to inside it. This instinctively causes them to open the clubface, to keep it from releasing or turning over through impact. This open clubface combined with the outside-in path produces a weak slice from left to right. If the player does manage to get his clubface squared or closed with this swing path, the result is a pull hook that starts left and keeps going that way.

If this is your problem, you need to retrain your thinking and the reaction of your muscles to get to that ideal inside-to-inside path. To do that, you may need an intermediate step. For a while you may be better off to think of swinging from *inside to outside*. That's not ideal, but it probably is the best way, temporarily, if you have been swinging at the ball from the other direction.

When you think of swinging from inside to out, your right elbow moves closer to your right side on the forward swing and you retain the angle between your hands and arms longer coming into impact. At first you may hit the ball to the right. Then, when you begin to sense the feeling of swinging the club into the ball from the inside, your hands will begin to release at the most efficient time, squaring the clubface at impact, and you will begin to draw the ball back on line.

This path eventually can cause some problems. You may begin to overwork your shoulders to get the ball started straight, or you may begin overworking your hands to hook the ball more. This usually brings the right hand too much into play, overpowering the left and causing disaster.

When you get to this stage—or hopefully before you do—you should start bringing your swing path back toward the ideal.

The path of that ideal swing is, from start to finish, straight back from the ball for a short distance, then inside,

*The club returns to the ball
from inside the target line.*

around your body and up on the backswing. At the start of
the forward swing, the plane of the swing lowers and your
arms and the club drop even more inside. The clubhead returns to the ball from inside the target line, goes straight
down the line for a short while and then swings back inside
and up on the follow-through. In sum, it's straight back, inside, around and up on the backswing, then from inside to
down the line to inside and up on the forward swing.

As you start to train yourself to swing on this path, you
should relate to the swinging of your hands and arms rather
than the movement of the clubhead. Later, as you internalize
these movements and develop more feel for the swing, you'll
begin to sense the location of the clubhead and the position

of the clubface at all times. But at the beginning, assume that if the arms and hands swing correctly, the club has to travel on the right path.

Simply relate to the two swings supported by the pivot of the body—on the backswing, the hands cock the club up while the arms swing it *laterally* and the turning of the body swings it *around* and behind you. On the forward swing, the reverse happens. If all this is done with proper pace in the correct sequence, without you doing anything to hinder the action, the inside-to-inside swing will happen.

Here are a couple of images that will help. Remember the halfway-back handshake position we described in Chapter Three? Imagine as you address the ball that there is somebody standing directly to your right. Extend your right hand and arm toward him as if to shake hands. Put both hands together as if gripping a club and do the same thing. Now do it again with a club in your hands. That's the position you want to be in at that point.

Now, at the top of the swing, visualize that your left thumb is pointing directly over your right shoulder, aimed straight down a line that is parallel to your target line.

If you build these sensations into your swing, your hands and arms will keep the clubhead and shaft where they belong going back. That makes it a lot easier to allow them to come forward in the right manner.

At this point, good players will reroute their arms and the club more to the inside, away from the target line and into a lower plane. You should do this, too, because it enhances your ability to swing forward into the ball from the inside.

After impact, the club-head goes left with the left arm.

Basically, this is done by the movement of the feet and legs while the shoulders do nothing to interfere with it. Then your arms can simply drop and swing the club through on the inside-to-inside path.

The important part of this motion is that as you swing through the ball and into your finish, you should feel the left arm and the clubhead moving left, back to the inside of your target line and around your body. The left arm folds at the elbow as it goes. But remember, the *clubhead* must go left with the left arm. This will happen when your hands release correctly through impact. If you think only of the left arm going left, you will tend to get the grip end too far in front of the clubhead, which will inhibit a good release and reduce your distance and accuracy.

As the clubhead moves left after impact, it also goes up. Remember the first swing—the hands cock, uncock and re-cock. As they recock in the follow-through, the club goes up. This recocking of the hands and the upward movement of the club accomplishes a full, uninhibited release and also helps the left arm fold correctly as it swings inward and upward.

Plane and Its Importance

Plane, as it applies to the golf swing, is simply the angle of your swing arc in relation to the ground. If you were to make a perfectly upright swing, the clubhead would swing on an arc at a 90-degree angle to the ground. If your swing were perfectly flat, the clubhead would swing around your body and never leave the ground.

The plane of *your* swing is influenced by your height and body type, by your posture and by the length of the club in your hand. If your upper body is properly tilted at address, your arms will be free to swing on a reasonably vertical plane, which is what we're after. Too flat a plane induces an outward movement of the shoulders and arms on the forward swing to get the club back on line, rather than the inward movement that we prefer…and that you should prefer.

The taller, more slender player generally will swing on a more upright plane. The shorter player, especially if he or she is heavily built, will have a flatter plane, more around the body. The player of average height and build usually has a plane that falls somewhere in between. So don't force yourself to swing on a plane that doesn't fit your body type. Also understand that your plane will be more upright with the shorter clubs, which have more upright lies, simply because your body is more tilted at address. Your plane will get a little flatter with the longer clubs in your hands.

Remember that there actually are two planes in every swing. Because you have, ideally, rerouted your arms at the top, your forward swing plane will be lower than the plane of your backswing.

Keep Clubface Square to the Path

Throughout the swing, the clubface should remain *square*. That's a term that is often misunderstood. It does not mean the clubface should be kept square to the target line. Again, that would require the physical impossibility of swinging like a Ferris wheel. It means the clubface should be kept square to the *path* and the *angle of the plane*. More specifically, it means the clubface should remain in the same relationship to the hands and forearms as it was at address. As the hands cock and the forearms rotate going back, the clubface will appear to be turning open. It is, but only to the target line. It is remaining square to the path and plane.

The opposite happens coming forward. The clubface appears to be closing as it comes into impact, then turning over as it swings into the follow-through. It is doing that, but only in conjunction with the rotation of the arms and the uncocking and recocking of the hands.

That makes it simple. As your hands cock the club up,

just swing your arms straight back, inside, around and up. Then your arms swing down from the inside to along the line as your hands uncock, back inside and up again as your hands recock. There will be no independent manipulation of the clubface and it will match your path and plane throughout the swing.

Keep Your Swing Center Behind the Ball

Your swing center is the center of the arc on which the arms and club are swung. Keeping it relatively constant and maintaining your balance are interrelated, because so many of the same swing concepts apply.

We prefer to think the head as the swing center, because it moves the least of any body part during the swing. If you keep your left eye focused on the top of the ball as we indicated in Chapter Two, the head will remain relatively stable throughout the backswing and through impact. Some teachers and players tell us that the sternum is the swing center, or that we should swing around the spine. These thoughts, we feel, can lead to problems, mainly because they tend to make you keep too much weight on your left side during the backswing. Because you're concerned with turning around a point that you're trying to keep very still, you may not get your upper body behind the ball at the top of the swing. You will tend to work off your left leg and may actually end up making a reverse weight shift, which tips your upper body ahead of the ball.

From there, your left leg obviously is going to have trouble moving toward the target to lead the forward swing, because there is too much weight on it. All you can do is fire and fall back to the right, which is the classic reverse weight shift.

Here's a better idea. It's the right leg and knee that should support the golf swing going back and starting forward, so your thought should be to *swing the left side of your body around the right leg and back again*. This provides a constant support for your swing and lets you stay in the same position relative to the ball that you were in at address.

With the right leg and knee supporting at the top of the swing, the left knee then has the freedom to move and lead the rest of the body and the arms on the forward swing. The left knee feels weightless at the top, a feeling that is most predominant with the driver and progressively less so as the clubs get shorter.

You also have turned your upper body nicely behind the ball or to the right, which is where you want it. In any activity in which you are trying to propel an object forward, you begin the motion from your right side, and this is particularly true in golf. And the farther you want to throw the object, or hit the ball, the more you want to get your weight to the right. Then you can create momentum in your swing by moving the left leg forward.

On the forward swing your weight must move to support the motion. You should feel that you are swinging around your *left* leg, the right arm rotating around the left side as you swing through impact and beyond. This keeps you from hanging back on your right side too long, which causes the arms to swing too much up and out instead of around your body.

In any event, you want to keep your swing center behind the ball through impact. You see some good players whose upper bodies move forward at the finish of the swing, but not until well after the ball has been struck.

For a while, concentrating on swinging around the right leg may promote a feeling of swaying, moving your upper body backward from the ball. As long as your right leg remains reasonably firm, your right knee does not straighten and you keep your weight to the inside of your right foot, this won't happen. If you keep your left eye focused on the ball, your head will remain pretty well fixed. Even if you do sway a little with the driver, we'd rather have you make the mistake at that end of the spectrum for the time being. At least you're creating a good, full motion and putting yourself in position to make a strong forward swing through the ball. Once you learn the feeling of getting behind the ball at the top and staying behind it through impact, you can start bringing your swing under control.

Stay in Dynamic Balance

Maintaining your balance and body control while you swing backward and forward is essential to effective shotmaking. Because it is so critical, we should take a look at how your weight actually shifts during the swing.

It does shift to the right foot on the backswing and to the left foot on the forward swing. But a lot of emphasis has been playing on getting to your left side as quickly as possible, and that really doesn't happen in a good swing. Yes, the left leg leads the forward swing and, yes, a lot of your lower body weight does go to your left foot and leg, but if you are to keep your upper body behind the ball at impact, you can't have all or even most of your weight to the left. Indeed, at impact, the position of your body is remarkably similar to your address position. With a driver, in fact, your swing center may have moved a little to the right or more behind the ball. That's because the club is swinging on a level to upward arc, and if the club is swinging up your head and swing center must move back and down as a counterbalance.

Players who try to shift too much weight to the left side *too soon* tend to get the entire body too much in front of the ball, working the upper body around and over the ball, which leads to disaster.

Instead of a weight transfer, we believe it is better to think of a *transfer of momentum*, a change of body position that creates the momentum of the club on the forward swing. Your left knee is moving toward the target, taking your lower body with it, and your right heel is coming off the ground, so you *feel* that your weight is moving to the left. What you are feeling in addition to the weight transfer is pressure on that left side. At impact, even though your right heel is off the ground, there still is some weight on your right side. That's what allows you to keep your upper body and your swing center behind the ball as your arms swing the club forward.

Your weight goes to the inside of your right foot at the

top of the backswing and returns to the *outside* of your left foot by the time of impact. Your right hip, which moved just slightly to the right on the backswing, has moved several inches toward the target by the time you reach impact. But the overall weight distribution of your upper and lower body hasn't changed much at that point. In fact, we believe that, even though your body positions change, your center of gravity doesn't change significantly from address to impact.

The fact that your upper-body weight mass remains relatively stable while your left arm swings forward and left creates the momentum that generates clubhead speed. Remember the crack-the-whip game you used to play as a child? If you were the anchor person, you dug in and maintained your position to send the person at the end of the line flying. That's just what happens in a golf swing. You keep the axis of your swing constant while swinging with the left arm to create the greatest possible clubhead speed. It's only after impact and after the ball is gone that the weight moves more fully to the left side.

A caution here. The weight *does* move almost fully to the left side as you swing into the finish. Trying to keep the weight back too long can be just as damaging as trying to get it to the left side too soon. The transfer of weight slows only momentarily at impact as the arms swing the clubhead through the ball, creating the crack-the-whip action. Then the transfer of momentum carries you onto the left side.

The Angle of Descent Changes With the Club

This is something you need to be aware of but don't need to worry about. The angle at which the club comes into the ball on the forward swing will change with the nature of the shot and whether the ball is on a tee.

For example, you stroke a putt with a pretty *level* swing. The putterhead comes up a little on the backswing and up a little again on the follow-through, but at impact it should be moving level with the ground. With the ball on the ground and an iron or fairway wood in your hands, you want to be swinging into the ball on a *downward* angle. This angle increas-

At impact, the putter is moving level with the ground...

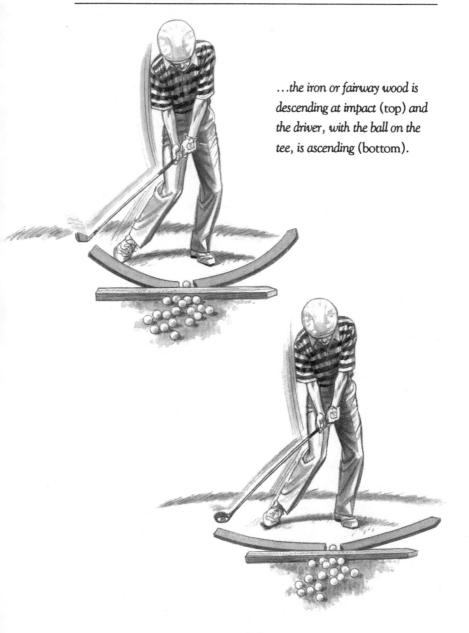

...the iron or fairway wood is descending at impact (top) and the driver, with the ball on the tee, is ascending (bottom).

es as the club gets shorter. It's a pretty slight downward angle with a fairway wood or long iron, and it gets steeper or more acute with the middle and pitching irons. That's why your divots are deeper with a 9-iron than with a 3-iron. With a 3-wood you should only be brushing the grass in front of the ball.

On the other hand, with a driver and with the ball on a tee, your clubhead ideally will have bottomed out and should be moving slightly *upward* at impact.

This change of angle, however, is a result of your ball position and setup at address. If you do that correctly, as we discussed in Chapter Two, it will happen naturally in the swing unless you do something to interfere with it.

Release Must Be On Time

Almost everyone we teach wants to know about release, what exactly it is. Actually, release just happens if you have done everything else correctly in the swing. Release means "to let go of," and that's what happens in the golf swing. You simply release or let go of that stored-up energy in the second lever, when you cocked your hands on the backswing, so that the clubhead arrives at impact traveling at maximum speed and with the clubface square to the intended line of flight.

As the arms swing forward from the top, the angle set between the left forearm and shaft will be retained well into the forward swing if there is no independent action of the hands. As the left forearm rotates counterclockwise and centrifugal force begins to work on the clubhead, the hands will respond to this weight buildup and the force of the second

With proper timing in a passive release, the hands, shaft and clubhead return to the starting position at impact.

lever, the club, will begin to be released. If your timing is proper, the angle of your wrist cock will be fully straightened, the shaft will be in line with your left forearm and the clubface will be square at impact. Then your arms and the club simply continue into the follow-through as we've described.

That's called a *passive* release, which means you don't have to think about it to make the clubhead arrive at the ball at the proper time and in the correct position. In essence, it returns to its starting position at impact.

The proper release, of course, depends on good timing. Visualizing a 200-meter dash around a curve helps us see how the club must be swung to get an on-time release. The runner in the outside lane has to have a head start. Otherwise he'd have to run farther in that lane than the man on the inside lane.

Our 200-meter dash starts at the top of the swing—actually, the preparation for it starts at the beginning of the backswing. The clubhead has traveled approximately 18 feet, the hands have gone about six feet and the waist has only turned a foot. That's why you need to start cocking the hands up, which in turn cock the clubhead up, early in the take-

Visualize the clubhead, hands and waist in a 200-meter dash to get an on-time release.

1.

2.

5.

6.

3.

4.

7.

*The whole swing comes
from combining vertical,
lateral and rotary dimen-
sions in a sequence that
fits your needs and pro-
duces an on-time release
at impact.*

3.

4.

7.

The proper pace, a feeling of unhurried, effortless power from start to finish, is the one factor above all that will give you an effective golf swing.

away. The clubhead has a lot farther to travel. Now, all these elements will travel those same distances returning to the ball. So, to get an on-time release, you must time the swinging of the club with the swinging of your arms with the turning of your body. The arms swing faster than the body turns and the hands eventually uncock to bring the clubhead roaring into the ball at maximum speed.

To make this happen, you need timing. You need the sensitivity to feel the golf club, and you need the time in your swing to release and square the club through impact, then allow the club to swing on past you with a free motion.

All of the elements we have discussed in this chapter—in this book, in fact—need to be internalized so you have a feel for them without having to think about them, and they need to be tied together with the timing that will make them work. That timing, as we have stressed, depends on swinging at a pace that you can control. When you put all this together, you will have a whole swing that will work when you need it.

So your practice goals should be related first to feeling the head of the club as you swing it. Then you need to develop a feel for the path of the club. Finally, work on feeling the face position as you swing the club back and through. At the same time, you should work on the pace that makes this happen.

On the golf course, you want to sense and feel the pace of your swing related to your target. The eyes sense the target, the hands feel the golf club and the feet feel the ground. Developing this sensitivity to the target, the golf club and the ground will help you build a swing that will let you play good golf for a lifetime.